Super Structures

Space Needle

by Julie Murray

Dash!
LEVELED READERS
An Imprint of Abdo Zoom • abdopublishing.com

3

Dash!
LEVELED READERS

Level 1 – Beginning
Short and simple sentences with familiar words or patterns for children who are beginning to understand how letters and sounds go together.

Level 2 – Emerging
Longer words and sentences with more complex language patterns for readers who are practicing common words and letter sounds.

Level 3 – Transitional
More developed language and vocabulary for readers who are becoming more independent.

abdopublishing.com

Published by Abdo Zoom, a division of ABDO, PO Box 398166, Minneapolis, Minnesota 55439. Copyright © 2019 by Abdo Consulting Group, Inc. International copyrights reserved in all countries. No part of this book may be reproduced in any form without written permission from the publisher. Dash!™ is a trademark and logo of Abdo Zoom.

Printed in the United States of America, North Mankato, Minnesota.
052018
092018

Photo Credits: Alamy, iStock, MOHAI p.8/1963.3119.103, p.16/2002.37.12569.6, ©Seattle Municipal Archives p.10/CC BY 2.0, The Seattle Public Library p.12/spl_gg_76640018, p.17/spl_gg_68810010
Production Contributors: Kenny Abdo, Jennie Forsberg, Grace Hansen, John Hansen
Design Contributors: Dorothy Toth, Neil Klinepier

Library of Congress Control Number: 2017960597

Publisher's Cataloging in Publication Data

Names: Murray, Julie, author.
Title: Space Needle / by Julie Murray.
Description: Minneapolis, Minnesota : Abdo Zoom, 2019. | Series: Super structures | Includes online resources and index.
Identifiers: ISBN 9781532123146 (lib.bdg.) | ISBN 9781532124129 (ebook) | ISBN 9781532124617 (Read-to-me ebook)
Subjects: LCSH: Space Needle (Seattle, Wash.)--Juvenile literature. | National monuments--Juvenile literature. | Architecture--building design--Juvenile literature. | Structural design--Juvenile literature.
Classification: DDC 725.9709--dc23

Table of Contents

Space Needle

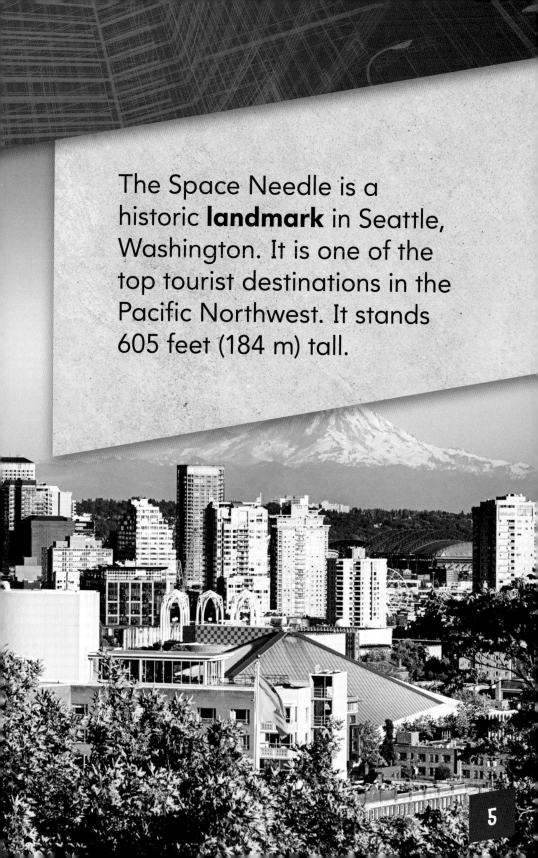

The Space Needle is a historic **landmark** in Seattle, Washington. It is one of the top tourist destinations in the Pacific Northwest. It stands 605 feet (184 m) tall.

It was built for the 1962 **World's Fair**. Planners wanted to show how skyscrapers may look in the future. More than 20,000 visitors went to the top each day during the fair.

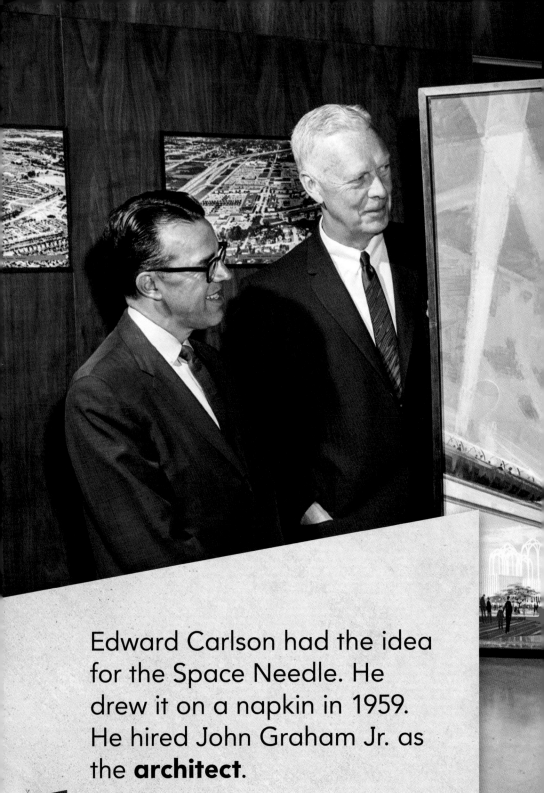

Edward Carlson had the idea
for the Space Needle. He
drew it on a napkin in 1959.
He hired John Graham Jr. as
the **architect**.

Building the Space Needle

Construction began April 17, 1961. A hole 30' x 120' (9m x 37m) was dug for the **foundation**. More than 460 trucks of cement filled the hole!

Crews built three steel legs at the base of the structure. A special crane was used inside the central tower.

A saucer-shaped structure was built on the top. A viewing deck is at 520 feet (158 m). A rotating restaurant is at 500 feet (152 m). It takes 47 minutes to complete one rotation.

America's
Space Age

WORLD'S FAIR

SEATTLE, WASH., U.S.A.
April 21 – October 21, 1962

CENTURY
2I
EXPOSITION

Construction ended in December 1961. It was called "The 400 Day Wonder" for the number of days it took to build. It opened on April 21, 1962, the day the **World's Fair** began.

The Space Needle Today

The Space Needle lights up at night. It changes colors for special occasions. It also has a fireworks show on New Year's Eve.

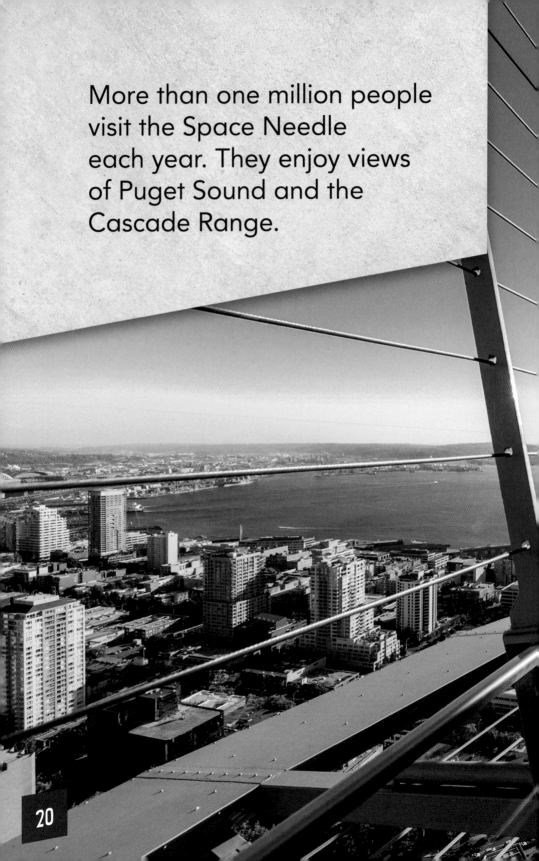

More than one million people visit the Space Needle each year. They enjoy views of Puget Sound and the Cascade Range.

21

More Facts

- In February 2017 the Space Needle was hit by lightning. Luckily, it has 25 lightning rods on the top to keep people and the structure safe!

- It takes 41 seconds to get to the top in an elevator. If you don't want to take an elevator, you will have to walk up the 848 stairs.

- The Space Needle had a $100 million renovation in 2017 and 2018. A glass floor was added in the restaurant and glass panels replaced the cage-like enclosure around the observation deck.

Glossary

architect – a person who designs buildings and directs their construction.

foundation – the stone or concrete structure that holds up a building from beneath.

landmark – a historic building.

world's fair – an international exhibition that showcases the industrial, scientific, technological, and artistic creations of the participating nations.

Index

architect 8

Carlson, Edward 8

construction 10, 13, 14, 17

features 14

Graham Jr., John 8

height 5, 14

materials 10, 13

New Year's Eve 18

opening 17

Seattle, Washington 5

viewing deck 14

world's fair 7, 17

Online Resources

Booklinks
NONFICTION NETWORK
FREE! ONLINE NONFICTION RESOURCES

To learn more about the Space Needle, please visit **abdobooklinks.com**. These links are routinely monitored and updated to provide the most current information available.